Twelve Walks
on the Lizard

Bob Acton

Tor Mark Press · Redruth

Published by Tor Mark Press, United Downs Industrial Estate,
St Day, Redruth, Cornwall, TR16 5HY
ISBN 0 85025 357 8
First published 1989   Second edition 1996
© Ivan Corbett Publishing, 1989, 1996

Printed in Great Britain by Burstwick Print
and Publicity Services, Hull

Introduction

This is a book of circular walks with contrasting coastal and inland sections. They range from about 2½ to 6 miles, and, despite a few steep slopes, all should be easily manageable by reasonably fit adults and children. The timings given assume a fairly leisurely pace. The relevant Landranger map numbers are given; having the map with you could increase your enjoyment, but the walks can be done from the book alone.

All the routes avoid roads where possible and keep to public rights of way, except for one concessionary footpath. The directions were accurate at the time of writing, but of course the landscape is constantly changing, and you may find that signposts have gone, fields have been ploughed or hedges removed. If you do encounter such problems, there is usually someone nearby to help. I should be pleased to hear, via the publisher, of any changes which would improve future editions.

The introduction to each walk gives information about parking, toilets, pubs, cafés, shops and telephones. Any special problems like particularly overgrown or muddy patches are also mentioned there, but remember that waterproof footwear is always advisable. A stick could also be helpful — and rainwear, of course!

I hope these walks will help you to enjoy this superb area, and that they will encourage you to explore further for yourself.

Bob Acton, January 1989

The Country Code

Enjoy the countryside and respect its life and work
Guard against all risk of fires
Fasten all gates
Keep dogs under close control
Keep to public footpaths across farmland
Use gates and stiles to cross fences, hedges and walls
Leave livestock, crops and machinery alone
Take all litter home
Help to keep all water clean
Protect wildlife, plants and trees
Take special care on country roads
Make no unnecessary noise

and in addition:

Go carefully near sea cliffs
Never trust the sea even in quiet weather

List of walks

1 and 2 Two circular walks based on Helford Village
  3 and 5 miles
3 Porthallow—Gillan—Porthallow 4½ miles
4 St Keverne—Porthoustock—Porthallow—St Keverne
  3½ miles
5 Coverack—Beagles Point—Black Head—Coverack
  4½ miles
6 Poltesco—Ruan Minor—Cadgwith—Poltesco 2½ miles
7 Lizard—Cadgwith—Lizard 4 miles
8 and 9 Two short coastal walks based on Lizard Town
  3 and 2 miles
10 Kynance Cove—Soapy Cove—Kynance Cove 3 miles
11 Predannack—Ogo-dour—Mullion Cove— Predannack
  4 miles
12 Poldhu—Gunwalloe Church—Cury—Mullion—Poldhu
  6 miles

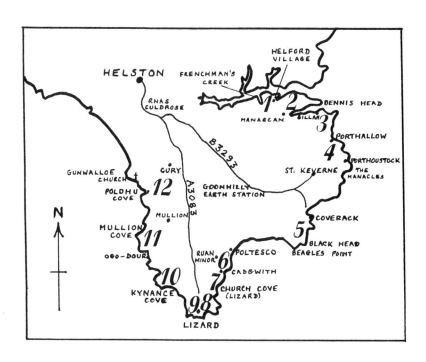

1~2   Two circular walks based on Helford Village

O.S. Landranger map 204
Walk 1: Helford Village — Frenchman's Creek — Helford Village nearly 3 miles. About 2 hours
Walk 2: Helford Village — Manaccan — St Anthony — Helford Village: nearly 5 miles. About 3 hours.
Or combine the two into one walk of about 7½ miles.

Helford is a 'picture-postcard' village, one-time haunt of pirates and smugglers, and these walks near it are superb, with wooded valleys and rich, undulating farmland. Walk 1 includes Frenchman's Creek, made famous by Daphne du Maurier, as well as a wood by the river and a little cove with a beach. Walk 2 links two old churches, one in the charming inland village of Manaccan and the other at the head of another beautiful creek, finally returning to Helford beside the Helford River. Walk 1 avoids roads except in Helford itself, but about a mile of Walk 2 is along a narrow road, sometimes quite busy in summer. Both walks include stiles and have muddy patches. On Walk 2 you pass through part of the Bosahan estate. The path here is concessionary, and it is important that walkers respect the ban the owners have placed on dogs. Helford and Manaccan both have pubs, shops, telephone boxes and toilets.

From Helston, drive to Helford via the A3083 and B3293 roads. Turn left 2 miles beyond Garras and then make for Newtown-in-St. Martin and Manaccan. You have to approach Helford from the east, and the car park is above the village on that side.

1 *For both walks:* Walk down towards the village. If you want to make use of the shop, café or pub, continue over the footbridge at the bottom; but for the walk, take the lane on the left, signposted to Manaccan, by the road bridge. You are soon walking up the valley with the stream to your right.

2 *For walk 2, turn to page 6.*   *Walk 1:* After about a quarter of a mile, take the right fork over the stream, crossing by a bridge with a small granite stile. After another stile into a field, go straight on beside the hedge on your right, and through the gate into Kestle farmyard. Keep to the left of the farmhouse. Two more gates bring you to a road.

3 Now take the path opposite, marked 'Frenchman's Pill' (= Creek). A short woodland walk brings you to the head of the creek, where you turn right. This National Trust path runs

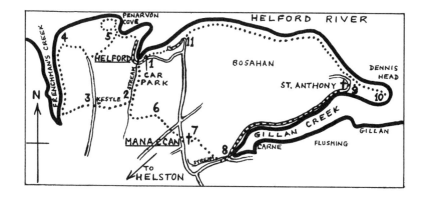

nearly the full length of Frenchman's Creek — a lonely, secluded spot where it's easy to imagine ships in hiding. After about half a mile, when the waterside path peters out, turn right, up steps. You now get good views of the Helford River, with Polwheveral Creek on the far side and the ancient Merthen Wood to the left of that.

4 After the stile, turn right on the lane, then fork right. Immediately beyond the cattle-grid go left, marked Pengwedhen and Penarvon Cove, and at the fork continue ahead, signposted Penarvon Cove.

5 At the cove, you have the option of making an attractive small detour. Turn to the left and go along this track for about a hundred yards until you reach a flight of steps on the left. Go up these. At the top, turn right past old stables and through a yard, and then look for the sign ahead, 'Woodland Circular Walk'. Go through the gate, then down to the right past a well, dug in 1926 to supply water for Pengwedhen House. (There are plans to re-route this path, so you may not see the well.) The path brings you to a tiny waterside chapel, erected about 1930 in memory of an uncle of the Misses Gerrans, who left this wood and the house to the National Trust in 1974. The chapel is dedicated to St Francis of Assisi, of whom there is a vivid sculpture inside. The walk continues just above the chapel and returns to the entrance gate. Back at the cove, cross the beach to the path on the right just beyond the stream. Follow the footpath signs, turn left at the lane, then right into the village, past the pub and back to the bridge and car park; or walk up the valley again to do Walk 2.

Walk 2: Keep to the main path up the valley. When you enter a field go straight on.

6 At the hedge turn right by the public footpath sign. At the road turn left and then immediately right (signposted 'Manac'!). Go straight ahead, with the hedge left, and over the stile into Manaccan. The name (pronounced 'M'*nac*'n'), apparently derives from the Cornish word for a monk. A chapel which once stood nearby may have been the cell of a hermit-monk. This part of Cornwall is called Meneage (said with a hard g), meaning Monkish Land. Turn right for the twelfth-century church with its famous fig tree growing out of a wall; it is reputed to be at least two hundred years old. The New Inn is a little further on.

7 The path leaves by the east end of the church, beside the vicarage. After a few yards, turn right, signposted Carne. After the first stile, go ahead with the hedge right. Another two stiles at field-corners bring you to a wooded valley, and the path continues through it. Cross the bridge and turn left on the road.

8 Take the first left turn, signposted St Anthony. This lovely road beside Gillan Creek can be busy, so use the path nearer the water where possible. The little Norman church is worth visiting. The granite in the tower seems to have been imported from Normandy, so there may be some truth in the legend that it was built by shipwrecked Normans who had vowed to build a church in honour of St Anthony if he saved them.

9 The path continues by a short flight of steps at the east (sea) end of the church. At the road turn left and then immediately right into the Bosahan Estate. At the acorn sign you could turn left for Helford, going diagonally uphill to the kissing-gate in section 10. But for a worthwhile short detour go straight on uphill towards the headland and at the top of the hill turn right. At the next acorn sign, with yellow arrow, turn left; then take the right fork through the remains of an Iron Age earthworks. This was re-fortified by the Royalists during the Civil War, and under the command of Sir Richard Vyvyan of Trelowarren held out against Fairfax's army until March, 1646. Next turn right at the footpath along the northern side of the peninsula to reach Dennis Head. The name, like 'Pendennis', means 'Castle Head'.

10 From there, return to the acorn sign with yellow arrow, and then follow beside the hedge on the right and through the kissing-gate by another acorn sign. After you have passed the two sea-marks beside a gateway, you cross two stiles, and then don't miss the right turn: the acorn sign is rather hidden. It takes you, via another kissing-gate, on to a pleasant, wooded section of the path and eventually brings you down to three small beaches, from each of which a private track leads up a small wooded valley to the house and five-acre gardens of Bosahan (pronounced 'B'zane'). The gardens, begun about a century ago, are well worth visiting; in most years they are open to the public on one or two occasions. (Details can be obtained from the *Gardens of Cornwall Open Guide* published annually by the Cornwall Garden Society.) As you climb away from the first beach, turn right by the acorn sign. At the second beach there is a boathouse. (You may hear, if not see, some of Bosahan's ornamental pheasants.) After the kennels, next to what looks like an old lime-kiln, the path becomes a surfaced lane.

11 At the road, take the right fork. Soon after 'The Old Pilchard Shed', the Coast Path is signposted left up some steps, and a kissing-gate on the right leads into Helford car-park.

3 Porthallow—Gillan—Porthallow

O.S. Landranger map 204
Just under 4½ miles. 2-3 hours. Can be linked with Walk 4.

A lovely walk through unspoiled countryside and along a quiet, beautiful part of the coast path. The latter is steep in places, so you would be wise to allow three hours for the complete walk. Porthallow (pronounced 'P'thalla' or even 'Pralla') is attractively situated where two valleys meet; it is still clearly a working village with many fishing boats on the beach. Gillan Harbour, at the other end of the walk, is utterly delightful — perhaps the more so because usually it is also utterly deserted. As you approach Gillan there are superb views north-east, including Falmouth and St Mawes, and in clear conditions Dodman Point, nearly twenty miles away. The inland half of the walk is easy but may be muddy, especially in the valleys; about half a mile is on quiet roads. Porthallow has an inn, shops, cafés, toilets and a telephone box, but you won't find any of these elsewhere.

Porthallow (grid reference SW 797232) is about 2 miles north of St Keverne. To drive there, take the A3083 south from Helston, turn left after Culdrose airfield on to the B3293, then follow the signs from the main square at St Keverne. At Porthallow you could park on the beach or in the village, for example opposite the phone box. Buses don't come here.

1 Walk up the road which passes the phone box. Where the road to Manaccan turns off to the right, go straight on, cross the stream, and turn right to pass in front of a terrace of houses. Just after the kissing-gate, take the lower path, which leads up through a pleasant valley. About half a mile later, after crossing a low wall among trees go straight on. Stepping stones take you over one stream, and there are a stile and a gate at another. Now the path bears left uphill. You cross a stile beside a seven-bar metal gate and then follow the hedge on your right, crossing the breeze-block wall by the steps in it.

2 Turn left at the road, passing Treglossick, a splendid-looking whitewashed farm complete with duckpond.

3 At the T-junction turn right. Notice the great variety of plant and animal life in the old hedges.

4 Where the main road turns left and a side road goes to Lestowder and Penare, continue straight on down a concreted lane signposted to Trewarnevas Farm and various houses.

5 About a quarter of a mile after the farm there is a clump of tall pines on the left. Go through the five-bar gate on the left here, on to a path that leads down through the wooded valley to Gillan Harbour.

6 To return to Porthallow, go up to the right on to the coast path. It starts rather steeply up steps. Soon you round Nare Point, with its observation post. The next stretch, around Nare Head, though perfectly safe, requires careful walking, because the path has fallen away in places. Later, you see the spire of St Keverne church on the skyline — a reminder of its value to sailors as a guide to avoid the Manacles; hence their name, *Maen Eglos,* Church Rocks. You will have a good bird's-eye view of Porthallow when you arrive.

You could do Walk 4 now, by going up the road past the Five Pilchards, and after about a quarter of a mile taking the path on the right to St Keverne. Follow the directions for Walk 4, in the order 6-8 and 1-5.

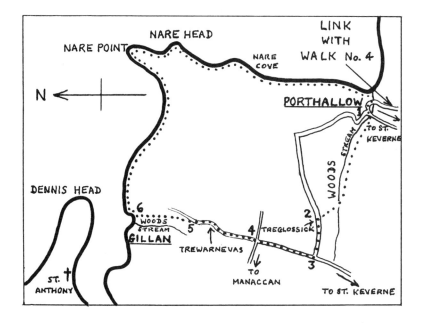

4 St Keverne—Porthoustock—Porthallow—St Keverne

O.S. Landranger map 204.
Just under 3½ miles. About 2 hours. Links with Walk 3.

This walk is based on one of the area's largest and most interesting villages, with a spacious, beautiful and fascinating church. First you go down a very pretty valley to Porthoustock (pronounced 'P'rowstock'), almost the only seaside village on the Lizard that most holidaymakers avoid (because of the ugly quarries and industrial buildings that mar the beach); yet it has several delightful cottages, and of course its very unpopularity has helped it to retain its authentic character. Next a section of the 'coast path' that is far from the coast but still gives some good coastal views; this brings you close to another seaside village, Porthallow, which you can visit if you wish, and from there possibly make this into an eight mile walk: finally, paths, mainly through fields, bring you back to St Keverne. The whole walk is easy, with no steep hills apart from a short stretch leaving Porthoustock, and not much road walking; there are also few stiles, but plenty of stone cattle-grids instead. There are telephones, toilets and cafés at St Keverne, Porthoustock and Porthallow. St Keverne and Porthallow also have shops and pubs.

St Keverne is about 2 miles north of Coverack. To drive there, take the A3083 to Lizard from Helston, turning left on to the B3293 south of Culdrose airfield. There is plenty of parking in the main square. For bus services from Helston, see the current timetables.

1 The path starts from the back of the churchyard, clearly signposted through a magnificent wrought-iron gate. Head for the sea, with the hedge on your left for the first 200 yards, then on your right. After two stone cattle-grids, cross the lane to a third one, where the path continues. Follow the hedge round to the left, then go straight on over the field to a stile and stepping-stones over a trickle of water. Now keep left, skirting the trees at first, then down into the valley — a lovely spot. Continue to a footbridge and stile, over a second bridge, then a cattle-grid with steps going down, and bear right, still following the stream although it's out of sight now.

2 At the road, bear left, and just past the second cottage take the footpath on the right. Walk for about 100 yards on the broad track, with the trees on your left; then take the higher, narrow path on the left beside the trees. Go up the steps in the wall, then through a kissing-gate. Just before a stile, a sign points left to the coast path — but to visit Porthoustock, carry on over the stile and down to the sea.

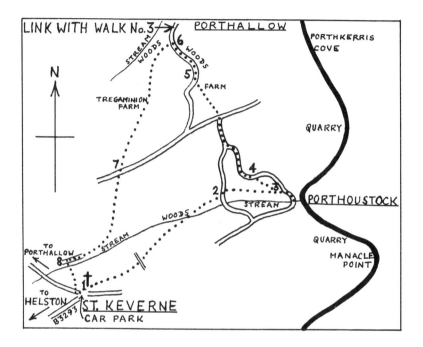

3 Return up the hill and past the thatched cottages to the coast path sign and go the way it points — rather steep and awkward for a few yards. After the cattle-grid go diagonally to the right across the field to another grid by the gate and a telegraph pole.
4 At the road, turn left, and at the junction follow it round to the right (signposted Porthallow and St Keverne) but at the sharp left bend go straight ahead along the path, following the acorn sign. After the stile you will pass a vineyard. Bear right beyond the farmyard as directed by the acorn sign.
5 Turn right at the road.
6 At the Porthallow sign, take the path on the left (signposted 'everne'!) — or, of course, continue down the road to visit Porthallow, returning to this path later. (To turn this short walk into a splendidly varied one which will probably fill most of your day, you could do Walk 3 now.) After the grid by the gate,

keep to the main path. When out in the open, bear left to the granite stile on the right of a gate. Cross the stream, then go uphill past the farm (Tregaminion), where you turn left by the farmhouse, then take the footpath signposted to St Keverne on the right. Go up the steps then bear left round a barn to a stone cattle-grid. Next cross the field to another grid on the left of a metal gate. (Look back for a fine view across Falmouth Bay to St Mawes, – and, in fine weather, as far as the St Austell china clay 'mountains' on the skyline.) Now keep by the hedge on the right, and after the next grid head towards St Keverne church, over another grid to yet another at the left-hand field corner. This brings you to a road.

7 Turn right and after some thirty yards turn left onto a path with a sign pointing back, announcing OOTPATH TO HALLOW. Walk by the hedge on the right. As you enter the wood, the path forks; go left down into the valley towards the church, then down the steps, over two grids by the stream, along the made-up lane and over the stile on the right of the five bar gate.

8 Take the footpath to St Keverne which is straight ahead as you cross the stile; it brings you over a footbridge, with the church ahead. At the road turn left to return to the village square. If you haven't already looked inside the church, please do so before you leave, and buy the blue guidebook to help you notice the many points of interest. Outside as well as inside, there is much evidence of the many shipwrecks on the nearby coast, including the tall cross near the north door commemorating (like the east window) the loss of the *Mohegan*, and the cannon overlooking the square, which came from a ship wrecked in 1809.

5 Coverack–Beagles Point– Black Head–Coverack

O.S. Landranger map 204
Just under 5 miles. About 3 hours

Based on Coverack, an attractive fishing village, this walk is through undulating farming country and along a coast as beautiful as it is impressive.

The first half of the walk is on roads and lanes, but only on the first mile is there any traffic. It compensates by being very level after the steep climb out of the village. The coastal section is much more strenuous especially if you explore the headlands. Coverack is well supplied with shops, pubs, toilets and telephones: use them whilst you can, as there are no facilities until you return. There are a number of farms and houses on the route where help could no doubt be obtained in an emergency.

Coverack has a long history going back to the thirteenth century. Pilchards were the main industry; they were caught, cured and exported from here. During the time of Queen Elizabeth I, taxes were put on the import of salt and the export of pilchards. This double blow to legitimate trade in Cornwall encouraged the development of a second industry – 'free trading', as it was discreetly called, which dealt in salt long before it dealt in brandy. The pilchard industry has alas now gone (and free-trading too) and the old salting houses have been converted into private houses and shops. The Paris Hotel is named after a liner which was stranded in May 1899. She was refloated, renamed *Philadelphia*, and stranded a second time at Rame Head. The Cornish coast is not always so forgiving.

Driving from Helston south on A3083, turn left south of Culdrose airfield on to the B3923 towards St Keverne. Then turn right to Coverack on the B3294. Out of season the most convenient car park is by the harbour; drive through the village and where the road turns sharp right go down to your left past the Paris Hotel and the old lifeboat house. This car park is very small, and in season you might save yourself a good deal of trouble by using the large car park as you enter the village. This adds half a mile at most to the round walk.

1 Go up the steep road above the harbour, by the harbourmaster's office, passing the village hall and the Methodist church. Keep climbing. After a while you reach the school; a hundred yards beyond that the road bears right, with a side turning going left.

Follow the road as it goes right, past Penmarth Farm. After a winding quarter of a mile, the road runs straight for half a mile past two camp sites. You come to a T-junction.

2 The footpath is immediately opposite and runs past a tin-roofed barn; the sign is partly hidden. The footpath brings you on to a quiet lane. Turn left and walk past Little Treleaver Farm.

3 At Ponsongath Methodist church turn left and pass Arrowan Common Farm. Shortly after reaching a very modest junction, take the right fork with the pond on your left. Go through the metal gate. (The honesty box is for drivers, not for pedestrians, though I am sure the farmer would be delighted to receive any additional donations.) This unmade track winds down to the coastal footpath, The Lizard lies to your right and the church tower you can see is at Ruan Minor.

4 A second metal gate brings you onto the coastal footpath at Carrick Luz. Here there was an Iron Age fort, its position bleak, but all the more easily defended. One archaeological opinion is that promontory forts like this were created by traders, possibly the Veneti from Vannes in southern Brittany, renowned traders whose navy commanded the western Channel in Roman times; if the natives turned unfriendly, the merchants could defend themselves long enough to make an orderly retreat by sea. You turn left to Coverack, a signpost marking the path. Apart from the hard climb out of Coverack, this has been easy walking. The second part of the walk is far harder. The local serpentine rock has been worn to a shine beside the first stile; there are similar traces along the remainder of the route.

5 After half a mile you drop down into the wonderful Downas Valley and Beagles Hole. A narrow wooden bridge leads you strenuously up the cliffs again. Tradition has it that along these cliffs one of the best known West Country pirates, John Avery, buried part of a great treasure he had captured from the Great Mogul of India at the end of the seventeenth century. There have been many unsuccessful searches. Should you prove more fortunate, please remember who told you first.

Walk up to Beagles Point, with fine views towards the Lizard. (A lower path gives the best sight of Beagles Hole but it is steep, especially when returning.) If you see ponies grazing on these cliffs, please do not disturb or feed them. Near the Point is a small wooden cross erected by the parents of an airman, one of four who died when their helicopter crashed here.

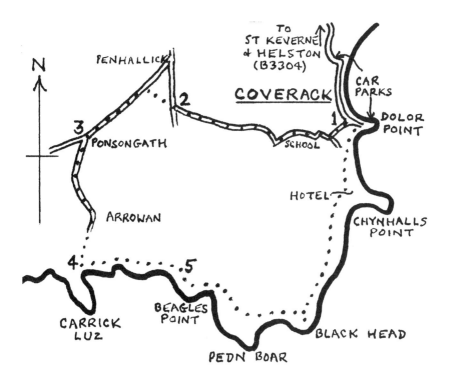

Soon after the stile by the National Trust sign is a fenced square where cables are tested by exposure to the elements. (I hope the same won't happen to you.) The next headland, with its coastguard lookout, is Black Head. The path out to the point involves some scrambling, but the tremendous views both east and west justify the effort. All around here, the contorted rocky outcrops among low gorse and heather are a memorable sight in late summer. You will find another stile by the sign Chynhalls Cliff (pronounced 'Sh'nalls'), then a bridge plus stile, and now you fork right. The next stile is beside a piggery. Keep left along a narrow path between hedges, then turn out onto a wide track; go straight on where another track crosses, ignoring the side-path later on the left. After the next stile you cross a stream, then go uphill past an old pump and follow the footpath sign to the right. At the road turn right (coast path sign and arrow); down steps then walk in front of the terrace of houses, and straight on down the road to the car parks.

6 Poltesco—Ruan Minor—Cadgwith—Poltesco

O.S. Landranger maps 203 and 204
2½ miles, approximately 1½ hours. Can be linked with
Walk 7.

Only 2½ miles long, this walk includes two lovely valleys, a water-mill still in occasional use, dozens of 'picture-postcard' cottages, a charming old church, one of the most attractive fishing villages in Cornwall, and a fine short stretch of the coast path. There is car-parking at Poltesco; Ruan Minor has shops, toilets, phone box and café; and Cadgwith has all those plus a pub, although the shop and café there are likely to be closed out of season. Part of the walk is on roads, but they are very quiet ones. The going in general is easy apart from steep hills at Poltesco and Cadgwith. There are several stiles. For a few yards the coast path is very close to the cliff-edge, so dogs and children would need to be kept in check, and perhaps you should think twice about doing this walk if you have no head for heights. The Lizard Field Studies Club has published a very interesting Nature Trail booklet dealing with this walk, available in local shops.

Poltesco is about a mile north of Cadgwith, and two narrow roads go down to it. Both lead into the National Trust car park.
1 Walk back up the road and take the first left turning, past Poltesco Mill. Notice the initials and date on one corner, and three dove-holes above a window. The leat feeding the overshot wheel is still in good order, and you may be able to see it among trees on the right a few yards up the hill. Continue up to Ruan Minor. The little church on the left, its tower festooned with Virginia creeper, is worth visiting, although like so many other Cornish churches it was somewhat insensitively restored in the nineteenth century.
2 At the T-junction, take the path which starts to the right of the phone box and runs beside the public conveniences.
3 At the road turn right and take the path on the right at the corner, past the Methodist Church. Go down the serpentine steps on to the narrow path. After a gate with a stile followed by another stile, bear left on the wider track leading down to the road.
4 Turn left and take the footpath on the left immediately beyond the bridge. This takes you straight down the valley, still attractive, despite the depredations of Dutch elm disease, into

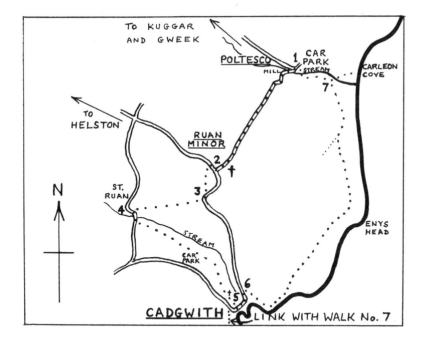

To KUGGAR AND GWEEK

POLTESCO

CAR PARK

1

MILL

STREAM

CARLEON COVE

7

TO HELSTON

RUAN MINOR

2

†

N

ST. RUAN

3

4

STREAM

CAR PARK

ENYS HEAD

6

5

CADGWITH LINK WITH WALK No. 7

Cadgwith. Notice the corrugated iron church (a chapel of ease, as often found in seaside villages whose mother church is well inland) which is quite a contrast to the almost too pretty cottages below, many of them built of serpentine rock. In some cases, the thatched roofs are chained to the walls.

5 At the bottom, you could, if you wish, turn right and do Walk 7 — an extra four miles. For this, walk up as far as Hillside and turn left at the coast path sign; now follow on from Section 6 in Walk 7. But to continue Walk 6, turn left, past the harbour. Notice on the left the old fish cellars with their open courtyard. Continue past the pub, and up the hill for a few yards as the road bends left.

6 Turn right (as indicated by a coast path sign on the opposite side) on to the path which runs up behind thatched cottages — a steepish climb, but the wonderful view of village and harbour amply repays you. The old black hut on your right just as the path turns to follow the coast was once used by coastguards; the theory is apparently untrue that originally it was for the 'huer' whose job was to watch for pilchard shoals and alert the fishermen. The first part of the path here needs special care; it runs close to precipitous drops, and the polished serpentine rocks underfoot can be slippery, especially if wet. The path to Poltesco is well-walked and clear. Apart from the fine sea views, there is an abundance of wild plants to look at, especially in crannies of the old walls. After the wooden fence, a bridleway joins from the left, but the coast path continues straight ahead.

7 Nearing Poltesco, fork right by the National Trust sign for a worthwhile short diversion down to the beach at Carleon Cove. Serpentine steps lead down to a footbridge, after which the path forks right again down more steps. The ruined buildings among the trees were connected with the serpentine industry which once flourished here. At the beach the three-storey warehouse of the main works is still largely intact. The round tower beyond it once housed a capstan for hauling fishing boats up the beach, and the warehouse was probably used as pilchard cellars before the serpentine works took it over and enlarged it in 1866. The factory also had an office building, four machine shops and a forge; power was supplied by a large waterwheel and a steam engine. The wharf was built to enable flat-bottomed barges to take the manufactured goods to ships for transportation to Penryn and Falmouth, and thence to London and overseas to satisfy a demand for ornamental serpentine shop fronts, mantlepieces and urns, following the inclusion of several serpentine pieces in the 1851 Great Exhibition. The factory closed during the 1890s, largely because of changing fashions and competition from foreign marbles. Many of the craftsmen set up small workshops in Ruan Minor and Lizard, some of which still survive.

8 Return to the main path and continue through a private garden to the bridge; turn right after the gate for the car park.

7 Lizard—Cadgwith—Lizard

O.S. Landranger maps 203 and 204
Just over 4 miles (about 2½ hours) including suggested
diversions. This walk can be linked with Walks 6 and 8.

Two attractive churches, a pleasant and unusual inland walk, partly on top of a Cornish double hedge, fine cliff walking and another chance to visit Cadgwith, plus 'The Devil's Frying Pan' and short optional diversions to a holy well and a lifeboat station. Even on the Lizard peninsula few other short walks offer so much. Most of the walking is easy: the only unavoidable steep parts are at Parn Voose Cove; there are stiles, but none awkward. Both Lizard and Cadgwith have shops, toilets, at least one pub, and phone boxes. The lifeboat station is normally open during daylight hours between Easter and October; on Thursday mornings a retired lifeboatman is usually available to show visitors over the boat itself. During the winter the buildings are open sometimes in the morning.

The walk begins at Landewednack Church Cove, half a mile east of the centre of Lizard town. Approaching from Helston, at the main square in Lizard turn left along Beacon Terrace; after a quarter of a mile fork right by the old cross (signposted Church Cove). There is a small car park on the left just pass the church. Buses run infrequently between Helston and Lizard.

1 St Winwalloe's church is worth inspecting inside, but probably it is the charm of its setting that most people remember. Go to the north side of the churchyard, furthest from the main gate. There you will find a path going down a few steps, then up a track between high hedges. After the stile at the top, continue ahead; then the path curves left into a valley. A gap in the bracken leads down stone steps. Cross the stream and wooden stile and turn left at once. You join a wider track to the left, which curves uphill; then the path continues sharp left, over the fence and stile by the footpath sign. Now follow the hedge on your right and cross another stile; here Grade Church comes into view ahead, with Goonhilly beyond, and further right is Black Head, near Coverack. Follow the next footpath sign pointing right (a stile through the hedge), and go on up the track to Trethvas farm.

2 Turn right in front of the farmhouse (sign to Cadgwith and Ruan Minor). After the stile on the left of a gate, the path runs along the top of the wall, or hedge as it is called in Cornwall. Eventually steps bring you back down to earth. Cross the stile by the gate ahead.

3 Turn left at the road, passing Anvoaze duckpond, and then right along the drive to Grade Church. Here the tower is 15th Century, built of serpentine and granite blocks, but the rest of the church is Victorian. Again it is the setting that one notices most — almost as different as can be imagined from St Winwalloe's.

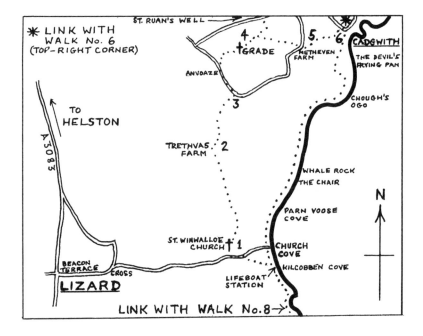

4 Go through the churchyard and cross the stile by an old gate at the north-east corner. Keep the hedge on your left. At the field corner you can if you wish cross the stile to visit St Ruan's Well, adding under half a mile to the walk. (The right of way is straight over the field; head for the nearest electricity-supply pole; continue in that line and you should find a stile near the end of an old hedge; turn left here and you soon reach another stile at the road. Cross the road, and a third stile brings you to the old holy well, still apparently a source of good water. Return to the point where you diverged from the main walk, and turn left after crossing the stile.) If you prefer not to visit the well,

don't cross the stile but turn right, get past the metal farm gate at the next corner, and walk along the path between hedges. Keep straight on to another metal farm gate, then over the road and through Metheven Farm.

5 Turn left among the farm buildings (sign to Cadgwith); a winding route among houses will bring you down into the village if you want to visit it, and you could then do Walk 6 if you wished.

6 Follow the coast path sign at Hillside, pointing right where the road down to Cadgwith turns sharply left. Walk up through Hillside's garden. After the bungalow on the right with a corrugated roof turn left (sign Inglewidden). Walk through the small parking space and cross the stile (by the National Trust sign) to The Devil's Frying Pan, where the natural bridge over the mouth of the inlet gives a sense of vast scale. From here till you reach the road at Church Cove you need no directions, but a large-scale map would help you to notice such things as Chough's Ogo (cave), Whale Rock and The Chair, another natural arch. You will catch glimpses of the lifeboat station ahead, and it's well worth a visit: just a short walk further along the coast path from the road to the church. (But note that it is also included in Walk 8.) The only snag is the number of steps to climb back from the boathouse! To return to the church, go up to the road above, over the cattle-grid and through a kissing-gate on to the church road. If you decide against visiting the lifeboat station, walk up the valley, past thatched cottages, at Church Cove.

8 ~ 9   Two short coastal walks based on Lizard Town

O.S. Landranger map 203
Walk 8 is just over 3 miles (about 2 hours)
Walk 9 is just under 2 miles (about 1 hour)
Or combine the two into a round walk of about 4½ miles
Walk 8 can also be linked with Walk 7

Visitors to the mainland's most southerly place miss the best of it unless they do walks such as the two suggested here. Walk 9, round Old Lizard Head, is very short and easy; apart from the splendour of the cliffs and coves close at hand, you have a good view of Kynance Cove and the best one of Lizard Point itself. Walk 8 is a bit tougher, since it is longer and includes some quite steep gradients, but if taken gently it should be manageable even by the least experienced walker, and there is much of interest on it, including two lifeboat houses, a lighthouse, a spectacular blow-hole and one of Cornwall's prettiest churches. If you decide to do the two walks as one, start with the directions for Walk 9. Lizard village has toilets, telephone boxes, shops and a pub — plus, incidentally, a fascinating little museum. Refreshments can also be obtained at Lizard Point and the Housel Bay Hotel. A booklet, *Illustrated Guide to Six Walks from Lizard Village*, produced by the Bristol University Lizard Project, is very informative, especially about the natural history of this area; copies may be available in the museum and some shops.

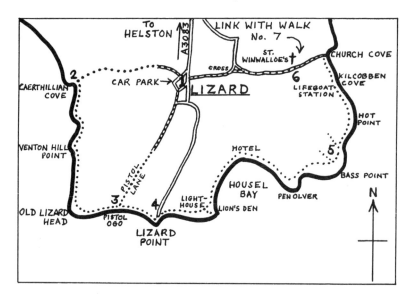

Buses from Helston stop at Lizard's main square or crossroads, and this is also the obvious place to park.

1 *To start Walk 9* go past the toilets on the west side of the car park (right as you approach from Helston), then straight on past Rocklands guest-house. The road soon becomes a track down an attractive valley to Caerthillian Cove.

2 At the bottom, turn left on to the coastal footpath, which starts up steps and takes you across two small streams. Don't miss the view back to Kynance. After a quarter of a mile, you will see a stepped pole as you approach Venton Hill Point; this is a rocket post, one of several around the coast formerly used to attach ropes to when breeches buoys were fired to ships in distress. After another quarter of a mile, the second seat looking out to sea is at Old Lizard Head, wrongly labelled Lizard Point on many maps. Once over the brow of the hill you have a good view of Lizard Point. Now the path descends to Pistol Ogo (probably meaning 'waterfall cave'; you need to get down to the foreshore — not easy — to see the waterfall).

3 Unless you want to continue with Walk 8 now, go straight up the valley instead of crossing the small wooden footbridge. This attractive bridleway, called Pistol Lane, leads into Penmenner Road and back to the centre of Lizard. (If you do wish to do Walk 8 now, cross the bridge and go up the steps; soon you will reach Lizard Point. Now read on from section 4 in Walk 8.)

To start Walk 8 from the car park, turn right by the pub (The Top House), continue past the hotel, and go straight on down Penmenner Road. After about a quarter of a mile, at a footpath sign, it becomes a track, which in turn leads to a bridleway called Pistol Lane. When you reach the coast path turn left over the footbridge and up the steps to the cliffs above Polpeor Cove. Notice how much of the cliff face is clothed with succulent plants (Hottentot-figs and smaller mesembryanthemums — escapes from gardens). The old lifeboat station closed in 1961.

4 At Lizard Point, go past The Wavecrest Café and The Most Southerly House to continue the coast path. The lighthouse is sometimes open to visitors: watch for the notice on a white gate in the lighthouse wall. Just by the lighthouse, take the well-defined side path on the right, and then at once turn right again on to a grassy path which leads to the chasm called The Lion's Den; this was a sea cave till its roof collapsed in 1847. Return to the main path. Approaching the Housel Bay Hotel you go down many steps to a bridge, then up steps and turn right as shown by an acorn sign. Continue round to Pen Olver, where there is a kissing-gate and a stile over a fence. At the narrow inlet just beyond, head for another stile and kissing-gate to the right of the castellated house. Next comes Bass Point, where there is a stile by the coast-guard lookout. The white line painted on the red brick wall here, in conjunction with another on the old Lloyds House above, acts as a guide to help seafarers avoid a submerged rock.

5 Just after the coastguard cottages, fork right by the acorn sign. The coast path winds for about half a mile before reaching Kilcobben Cove, where the present Lifeboat Station is. From here the path soon brings you down into Church Cove. Here turn left up the valley and past the thatched cottages to Landewednack church (St Winwalloe's), set very attractively among trees, though sadly the elms have succumbed to disease. This church is said to be where the last sermon in the Cornish language was preached.

6 Unless you're ready for more walking (in which case Walk 7 beckons!) return from the church by the road into Lizard. Ignore all footpath signs and the right fork in the road; join the main road (notice the old cross on the right at the junction) and continue past the school and along Beacon Terrace to the car park. Roughly opposite the Beacon Stores is where a beacon is lit on occasions such as the Armada anniversary in 1988.

For details about visiting the Lifeboat Station, see the introduction to Walk 7.

10 Kynance Cove—Soapy Cove— Kynance Cove

O.S. Landranger map 203
About 3 miles. 1½ to 2 hours

Kynance is the most famous beauty-spot on the Lizard coast, and has few rivals anywhere; this walk will help you appreciate it to the full, because by going a little way inland you discover how featureless this place would be without the erosive effects of water — streams as well as sea. The valley above Soapy Cove is very attractive, and the Kynance valley is famous for its birds. When I was last there, two people armed with binoculars enthusiastically reported several ringed plovers and a merlin. The high moorland is favoured by many species of butterflies, and reputed to support more types of wild heather than anywhere else in Britain. Predannack airfield is nearby, busy with helicopters and light aircraft, though on Sundays there will probably only be gliders. There are no roads or stiles on this walk, but some patches inland are rather boggy. The coast path includes one steep climb and one steep descent. There are toilets at the Kynance car park and a café at Kynance Cove, the latter open only in season.

The car park above Kynance Cove is signposted on the right of the A3083 just before you reach Lizard town.

1 From the further of the two parking areas, take the path at the extreme right-hand corner of the field — *not* the path by the flagpole, which would take you down to the cove, leaving you to walk up again. Turn left on to the track. Soon you reach a dip, and as you come to the top on the far side, take the grass track on your right, marked by two stone boulders.

2 Turn left at the public footpath sign which you soon come to. It leads down to a rather wet patch. Cross the stream, go through the gate, and then fork left by another footpath sign. At first the path is rather overgrown with gorse. Take the lower track, which curves left and right several times on its way to the clifftop. On the right you pass a relic of World War II when the airfield stretched as far as this: a screening wall intended to protect parked planes from enemy attack. Go straight on to the gap in the hedge, and turn right on the track you now come to. This runs between hedges to Kynance Farm.

3 Just before reaching the farmhouse, turn left and go down the valley, with its tiny stream and natural rock-gardens, to the

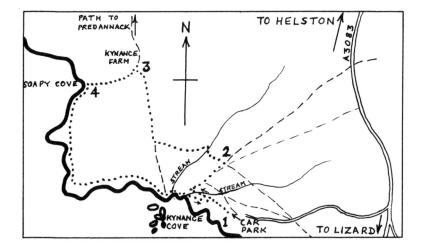

miniature gorge at the bottom, known as Soapy Cove because soapstone (steatite, French chalk) is obtained here.

4 Cross the stream and follow the coast path to the left — a steep climb. You soon reach the ominous cleft called Pigeon Ogo (cave), whose sheer black sides are lit up by flecks of orange lichen. Kynance itself is superb in all conditions, but best of all on a sunny day when the tide is low enough to reveal the white sands at the foot of the multicoloured rocky outcrops. Signs guide you down the steep descent to the cove. Return to the car park by way of the steps by the side of the café. This path joins the track on which you started. As an alternative, you can cross the beach at low water and climb over the rocks to further steps and a well-made path back to the flagpole.

11 Predannack—Ogo-dour— Mullion Cove —Predannack

O.S. Landranger map 203
A little under 4 miles. About 2¹/₂ hours

The clifftop part of this walk is very spectacular but is much less strenuous than many, with one moderately hard climb and one steep descent, so families with children should be able to manage the whole walk. Mullion Cove is a breathtaking place (mainly in the figurative sense) and this walk provides the best possible approach to see it in all its grandeur. A short diversion near Predannack leads to a small waterfall tumbling into a black cave. In co-operation with the National Trust, local farmers are using the cliff top as grazing land, partly with the aim of removing the coarser grasses which have suppressed wild flowers and other small plants, some of them rare elsewhere in Britain; so it is especially important that walkers with dogs should keep them under control. The view extends as far west as Gwennap Head near Land's End. The inland half of the route is easy and pleasant, traversing heathland and fields, with glimpses of the sea and sweeping inland views. It is a region of contrasts: near the end you pass a prehistoric burial mound and an ancient Cornish cross; in the distance behind the cross are the giant saucers of Goonhilly Earth Station, and overhead there will probably be a helicopter from Culdrose or the smaller airfield which skirts the cliffs here. Mullion Cove has toilets and a small café open in season, plus a gift shop. For the rest of the walk, you're out in the wilds.

Drive south from Helston on the A3083 Lizard road; Mullion Cove is signposted on the right after about 6 miles. Follow the B3296 through Mullion village, but where it curves right downhill towards the cove, take the minor road on the left, signposted Predannack. Ignore the right fork at Tenerife Farm, about a mile along the road. Finally you reach a National Trust car park. A few buses run from Helston to Mullion village; please check current timetables.

1 From the car park, follow the sign to Predannack Cliff, passing through Windyridge Farm buildings. Don't miss the right turning soon after, signed Footpath to cliff. Cross the stile by the gate, and soon you will come to the coast path. Turn right on to it. A few yards on, you will see a stile over the fence to your left; cross this and go down to the lowest easily accessible point to see the caves and waterfall at Ogo-dour Cove (Cornish for 'cave of the waters'). When I was there, in

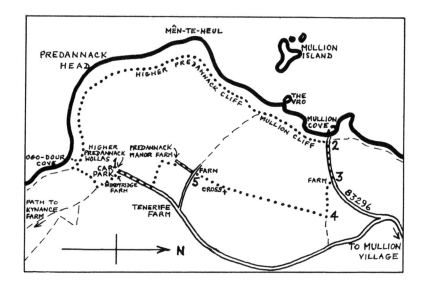

mid-September, there were also several mushrooms the size of dinner-plates but I can't guarantee those for everyone! Return to the main path. After the stream, a steepish climb; then a stile, after which the path curves left around Predannack Head. (Predannack derives from *Bridanoc,* meaning British. Probably the name was originally applied to Lizard Point, the first British headland many sailors would see. Locals pronounce the word as 'Pradnick'.) Go a little way inland again to cross the stile over the fence. As you approach Mên-te-heul Point you get your first sight of Mullion Island and Cove — the latter, unfortunately, dominated by a huge hotel, like Polurrian and Poldhu Coves beyond it. The ponies up here on Higher Predannack cliff seem to be omnivorous: I put my back-pack down in order to photograph one pony apparently eating gorse, and turned round to find another chewing the bag! Now comes a fairly stiff climb up to Mullion Cliff. Keep near the cliff-edge unless you're afraid of heights, to get the best views of the Vro (a sheer-sided islet close to the cliff) and of Mullion Harbour. The harbour was built in the 1890s, partly to help with the shipping 'up-country' of crabs and lobsters, following the failure of the pilchard shoals. The descent to the harbour is steep. Head for the stone winch house at the top of the slipway; the path goes round behind it to the right. The winch house is older than the harbour walls. Other buildings around the harbour include a net store and a fish cellar.

2 When you are ready to continue, walk up the road. (The toilets are up here, on the right by the gift shop.)

3 Just past the shop, take the public footpath on the right — a wide track on the left of farm buildings. Ignore the three right turnings, to private houses.

4 Cross the stile on the right between two farm gates, by a footpath sign. Walk by the hedge on your left, crossing several low stiles. The path becomes an alleyway among gorse and low trees. Out in the open again, it continues by the hedge on the left and over four more stiles. A few hundred yards away to the left here is the site of Wheal Unity, a very productive copper mine for nearly two hundred years before its closure in 1919. At the third stile is a Cornish cross. The fourth brings you to a farm, Bosvean.

5 Go straight ahead up the road towards Predannack Manor Farm and take the footpath on the left just before you reach the farm. Keep near the hedge on the right, passing the farmhouse. Cross over the stile at the corner and continue up the path straight ahead. This takes you to another stile; go over that, cross the field ahead to two more stiles, and then continue with the hedge on your left to one last stile, at the road. Turn right for the car park.

12 Poldhu—Gunwalloe Church—Cury—Mullion—Poldhu

O.S. Landranger map 213
6 miles. About 4 hours

Three old churches in contrasting settings are on this walk, which is mainly inland but includes a very fine stretch of coast and three good beaches. About two miles is on roads, one of which is busy in summer, but please don't let this put you off what is a most attractive walk. There are several stiles and slopes, but nothing very strenuous. It would be better to wear trousers rather than shorts, because there are a few overgrown patches. Cury has a shop and a pub; Mullion is a large village with all the usual facilities.

To drive to Poldhu Cove, leave Helston on the A3083 and turn right soon after passing RNAS Culdrose; the road is signposted to Cury and Poldhu. Poldhu, about three miles from the turning, has a large car park. Check current timetables for buses.

1 Go up the road on the north (right as you look out to sea) side of the cove. Soon you can walk on the cliff top — but please beware of crumbling edges. Before long you descend into Gunwalloe Church Cove. Cross the beach to the church and its separate tower, which are very nearly on an island: a wall fends off the sea to the north. Notice the inner door at the main entrance: the paintings of apostles are from a Portuguese ship wrecked here in 1527. Outside at the south-east corner is an old Cornish cross.

2 Leave by the main gate and walk a few yards up the road towards the farm, which is on the site of Winnianton Manor, one-time seat of the Carminows, whose estates included most of S.W. Cornwall at the time of Domesday. Take the grass track on the right, go over the bridge, and cross Mullion Golf Course. The track ends at the Poldhu-Cury road.

3 Turn left. Beware: the traffic here can be fast. After nearly a mile you will reach Cury church. Inside, notice particularly the squint which allows sight of the altar from the south transept; the low window in it was probably for the benefit of lepers excluded from the service.

4 Leave the churchyard by the south gate, near another old cross, turn left and at the main road turn right. After about a quarter of a mile, just past the main blocks of houses, turn right

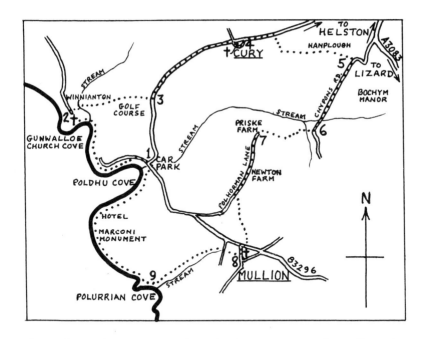

through the farm gate on the left of 'Gone to Earth'. Follow the hedge on the right; ignore the stile at the corner: turn left and keep following the field edge towards a farm (Nanplough), crossing three stiles, the last of which is close to the farmhouse. Here you go steeply down beside the wall on your right — care needed. Go straight down, through a gate, cross the bridge with a gate at each end, and now the path goes up to the left. A stile to help you cross the barbed-wire fence is on the left of the low embankment. The path goes up into the field and straight across the centre, but if it is planted go round the edge to the right, turning left twice. About 100 yards after the second corner is a stile; if this is too overgrown continue till you reach a gateway on the right. Go through this and follow the field edge left; at the second corner is a metal gate and on the left a stile. Take care as you cross this — or use the gate.

5 Turn right onto the road. Soon you pass the entrance to Bochym Farm, and Bochym Manor can be seen in the valley. It has a huge mulberry tree, and also reputedly a ghost. Cromwell destroyed the original house because its owner supported the Royalist cause. Continue down past Lampra Mill and cross the bridge. Ignore the path on the right by the bridge and go up the hill.

6 At the left bend turn right on to a path which goes down among trees, over a rickety bridge, and straight on beside a granite post by a rusty wrought-iron gate. After the gap in the barbed-wire fence the path becomes a sunken lane which soon goes uphill. Keep to the main track, bearing left. Cross the stile and turn right. As you approach Priske Farm, go through the gate.

7 Now turn left. Continue on this track past Newton Farm. A few hundred yards on, there is an old stone cattle-grid in the hedge on the left. Go over this and cross the field towards Mullion church tower. From the stile, walk up the field to the hedge-corner. Keep the hedge on your immediate right, and this will bring you to the road and toilets. The footpath opposite leads to the 'Old' Inn, and beyond that the church. Here notice the woodwork: the black pews with marvellously preserved carvings which were protected from Cromwell's men by being planked over; the south door with its dog-hole; and the north door, visible only from outside, probably 900 years old. The holes in it are where rusted nails fell out.

8 Leave the churchyard by the main gate on the south-west side, and take the footpath to Polurrian Cove on the left of Mullion House, opposite; continue straight on across the road at the T-junction, down steps and follow the signpost past La Flouder Thatch. After the stream fork left for the beach, which is smallish but in a lovely setting.

9 Go up the coast path on the right to Polurrian. The left fork next leads to a headland with fine views; bear right to continue along the coast. Before the Poldhu Hotel comes the monument commemorating Marconi's radio experiments here between 1900 and 1933. After the quite strenuous section down into Poldhu, the path emerges on to the road from the hotel to the beach and car park.